Mrs Boffy's Dreadful Day

Contents

Chapter One

MRS BOFFY'S HOROSCOPE

Mrs Boffy woke up one morning with the awful feeling that it was going to be a very bad day.

'Oh my goodness,' said Mrs Boffy to herself as she sat up in bed. 'I don't like this at all. Not at all.'

As if to make matters worse, the tea-making machine hadn't worked. And the moment she stepped out of bed to go into the kitchen and put the kettle on, she trod on Peterkin's tail.

'Haaaaaaaaa!' hissed Peterkin furiously, leaping up with a snarl, his fur standing on end in spikes. Until then he had been sleeping soundly on the fluffy rug beside Mrs Boffy's bed, dreaming of fish and mice.

'Oh, I'm so sorry, Peterkin!' cried Mrs Boffy. 'I didn't mean –'

But Peterkin had gone. Vanished in a flash. And although Mrs Boffy couldn't see him, she knew exactly where he was. Sitting on top of the curtain rail. Sulking. She could see the curtains moving, even though the window was closed. He would probably stay up there for hours. Mrs Boffy sighed. It really *was* going to be a bad day.

However, she managed to make a pot of tea (a bit strong) and two slices of toast (a bit burnt)

then sat down in her dressing gown and slippers to read the paper. Starting with her horoscope.

The person who wrote the horoscopes every day was called Raymon Romanski, and he was hardly ever wrong. Once he had even predicted an unexpected visit from Aunt Belladonna, so that Mrs Boffy was able to arrange to be out.

As Mrs Boffy started to read, she groaned aloud. 'Not one of your best days, I'm afraid, my dear,' said the horoscope. 'To begin with, nothing will go right. You will have a problem with one of your toes. And I do fear that you are going to break something precious. However, things might get better towards sunset.'

'Well, I certainly hope so!' exclaimed Mrs Boffy. And just for a minute she wondered whether to go straight back to bed and stay there. Until tomorrow. Or even the day after. But then, 'No,' she said firmly to herself. 'What will be, will be. However awful, I must see this thing through.'

After breakfast, Mrs Boffy put on her favourite hat and her most comfortable shoes (remembering the toe). And leaving Peterkin still sulking invisibly on top of the curtain rail, and Ragtag the donkey grazing in the orchard, she went into the village to consult Madame Marguerita, the Fortune Teller. Mrs Boffy hoped that Madame Marguerita might be able to tell her a little bit more.

Madame Marguerita had long, light brown hair and wore red velvet trousers and blue flip-flops and a navy tee-shirt with 'University of Warwick' printed on the front in white.

'Oh, you poor dear,' said Madame Marguerita sympathetically when she heard of Mrs Boffy's horoscope. 'Well, let's take a look at the tea leaves first, shall we?'

Fortunately, Madame Marguerita had only just finished breakfast herself, so there was still some tea in the pot with plenty of good, thick, soggy leaves which immediately sank to the bottom of the cup. Pouring the tea down the sink, Madame Marguerita suddenly tipped the cup upside down upon a saucer. Then she lifted it up and peered closely at what was left.

'Hmmm,' she said, after a minute. 'I see visitors. Three of them. All friendly.'

'Oh! That will be William, Ben and Mary!' exclaimed Mrs Boffy in delight. Things weren't going to be nearly so bad, after all.

'There seems to be a large, grey cloud following them, though,' said Madame Marguerita, frowning. 'Oh dear, perhaps it's going to rain!'

'Perhaps,' said Mrs Boffy, who didn't believe anything was quite as simple as it looked. 'Is there anything else you can tell me?'

Madame Marguerita thought for a moment. 'I could try the crystal ball,' she said. 'Sometimes it picks up even the faintest vibes.'

Taking the milk and the marmalade, the toast and the tea-cups out to the kitchen, Madame Marguerita fetched her crystal ball out of the cupboard and placed it upon the table on a square of midnight blue velvet. Then she drew the curtains and sat down.

In the dim cottage, the two of them waited. And waited. And waited. Then, with a tut of annoyance, Madame Marguerita seized the misty ball and shook it hard. Mrs Boffy half expected to see a whirl of white flakes, like a snowstorm in a paperweight.

'Stupid thing's on the blink,' explained Madame Marguerita, replacing it upon the velvet. 'I really shall have to get it re-charged. New

ones are almost impossible to come by, you know. If they're the real thing, that is . . .'

'Look!' cried Mrs Boffy. Inside the crystal, something was happening. The mist which had been very still, suddenly began to move gently around in a soft kind of swirl. Then, just as suddenly, it lifted. Leaving something showing quite clearly in the middle of the ball. One single, solitary thing. A tiny white flower.

'Oh!' breathed Mrs Boffy, turning quite pale.

'Hmmmm,' said Madame Marguerita, not noticing. She peered hard at the flower. 'A white poppy. *Meconopsis* something.'

'*Meconopsis haegtesse*,' whispered Mrs Boffy. A sudden chill gripped her. This could indeed be the beginning of a very bad day. Not only for Mrs Boffy. But for the whole of Hag's Ditch as well.

Chapter Two

BEN'S BAD NEWS

Mary and William were outside William's house when Ben arrived. They had already started discussing what to do that day.

'There's a fair on the common,' said William. 'It's got a smashing new ride called the Jelly Wobble.'

'Ugh!' shuddered Mary. 'That sounds awful! I'd be sure to be horribly sick! No, I'd rather –'

But she didn't get time to say any more, because there was Ben, hurtling towards them like a comet gone mad.

'Hey, listen, I've got some terrible news!'

panted Ben, skidding to a halt. 'It's about Hag's Ditch! And I think we'd better go and tell Mrs Boffy right away!'

'Good!' said William and Mary together. 'That settles *that*, then.'

And without more ado, they set off towards the village as fast as they could go.

All the way home from Madame Marguerita's, Mrs Boffy worried about the appearance in the crystal ball of the *Meconopsis haegtesse*. She hoped it didn't mean what she feared it might. The only thing to do would be to keep her ears and eyes wide open for the first sign of trouble. And mind how she dusted her favourite ornaments. Perhaps she would leave them till tomorrow.

'What will be, will be,' said Mrs Boffy again to herself. 'I've just got to bide my time, and wait.'

However she couldn't help feeling so nervous after a while that she jumped a mile when the pixie doorknocker gave a sudden sharp tap. Opening the door a little crack, she peeped round. To her joy and relief, Ben, William and Mary stood there.

'Oh, come in, my dears!' exclaimed Mrs Boffy. She stepped back invitingly. 'I knew you were coming!'

The children didn't ask how. After all, Mrs Boffy *was* a witch. That was precisely why they had come to see her. So that she could do something about the Road. Before it was too late.

'A *what*?' cried Mrs Boffy, when Ben had told his story. She could hardly believe her ears. 'They're going to build a Road? Cutting off a corner of the school playground? Widening Main Street? Going right across Farmer Dale's fields? Behind Buttercup Cottage? And straight through the *middle* of Hag's Ditch? Good gracious, no! That was the one thing which must not be allowed to happen – not now – not ever . . .

'It's true,' said Ben. 'Somebody my dad knows told my dad yesterday. This person works there. At the scrap metal factory. They're the ones who want to build the Road.'

'But why can't they build it somewhere else?' asked Mrs Boffy.

'Because the only other suitable place is right across the bottom of the factory owner's garden,' said Ben. 'And he doesn't want it there.'

'I'm not surprised!' exclaimed Mrs Boffy sarcastically. 'That scrap metal factory – I might have known. The people of Hag's Ditch have had trouble with them for years!' And for the second time that morning she reached out for her hat.

'Come along, my dears,' she said. 'We might be able to stop this in a . . . well . . . quite *ordinary* way, if we catch it in time. And tell the right people.'

'Who?' asked Mary.

Mrs Boffy thought for a minute. Then, 'Mrs

Pitts,' she said with a smile. 'There's nobody quite like Mrs Pitts for *organising* things.'

Mrs Pitts was in the garden of her house in Hag's Ditch searching for the Himalayan poppies she had sown, most carefully, that spring. As she crouched on hands and knees glaring angrily at the empty place where the magnificent blue blooms should have been, she grumbled to herself.

'Not a single seedling in sight!' she muttered. 'Just wait till I get on the phone to these people who sold me the packet! I'll make their ears tingle! I'll teach them to bamboozle me! I'll –'

Mrs Pitts stopped. And froze to the spot. Because all of a sudden she felt the most queer feeling. That she was being watched. And turning slowly round, she discovered that it was perfectly true.

Mrs Boffy, Ben, William, Mary, Ragtag and Peterkin (who had forgotten his sulks the moment the children walked in) were looking down at her over the hedge.

'I'm terribly sorry to interrupt you, Mrs Pitts,' began Mrs Boffy apologetically. 'But it's really *very* important. Ben, dear, *do* tell Mrs Pitts exactly what you told me just now.'

So Ben repeated his story about the Road. And as he did so, he couldn't help enjoying the effect it was having on Mrs Pitts. First she went quite red. Then her ears and cheeks turned purple. She seemed to swell up, all over. So much so, that Mary became quite alarmed. She was sure Mrs Pitts was holding her breath, and that if she didn't let it out soon she would go off with a –

Just in the nick of time, Mrs Pitts released her breath with a hissing kind of snarl. Her eyes flashed sparks of anger. Her fists clenched at her sides. As if she were getting ready to bop somebody on the nose. Ben took a hasty step backwards, just in case.

'I have never heard anything quite so PREPOSTEROUS!' shouted Mrs Pitts at last. 'Do these scrap metal people *really* think we will allow this to happen? Why, we have only to speak to the chairman of the council –'

'The chairman of the council wants them to build the Road,' said Ben. 'When they voted for it in the council, he voted twice.'

At that, Mrs Pitts turned positively green. She ground her teeth, and her eyes simply whizzed

round in her head. She was so furious that she didn't even notice Ragtag quietly munching the heads off her lace-cap hydrangea, nor Peterkin earnestly digging a large hole right in the middle of the Himalayan poppy bed.

Chapter Three

THE MEETING

Within minutes, Mrs Boffy, Mary, Ben and William had been swept inside Mrs Pitts' house to listen to her on the phone. The first person she rang was the Reverend Mr Wigglesworth.

'I'm holding an urgent meeting in my house!' shouted Mrs Pitts. 'Something of TREMENDOUS importance has come up and you are needed *right away*!'

The phone said something. Very meekly.

'What?' screamed Mrs Pitts. 'In the bath? What kind of an excuse is that, my good man? You have no *business* to be having a bath at a time like this! Wrap a towel around yourself and get over here THIS MINUTE!'

When Mrs Pitts was in a mood like that, nobody, not even Granny Dickens, liked to say no. So it wasn't long before her house was full of people. Quite overflowing, in fact. Even the

Cheesemans had ridden across on their badly behaved ponies and tethered them on the lawn.

'That scrap metal factory didn't ought to be built there in the first place,' grumbled Farmer Dale. 'Near to a village like Hag's Ditch. Nasty noisy smelly ugly old thing it is. Frightens the life out of my hens, sometimes, all they bangs and crashes coming from it.'

'Only when the wind is in the east,' said Miss Drewitt primly. 'Do let's be fair, Farmer Dale. However, I do agree it was quite ridiculous of the planning people to allow a hideous great factory to be built in a lovely rural area such as ours.'

'Spooks the ponies every time they have to pass the horrid place!' boomed Mrs Cheeseman. 'Buck and rear like mad things! Isn't that so, Cheese?'

'Yes, Mum,' agreed Miss Cheeseman, wondering when Mrs Pitts was going to offer coffee and biscuits all round.

'Well, it's no good grumbling about that now,' said Mrs Featherly, sensibly, 'because it's here to stay. The thing is, how do we stop this wretched Road?'

While they sat drinking and all talking at once,

Mrs Boffy began to have the strangest feeling. It was in one of her hands. The left one.

'Oh my stars and goodness,' said Mrs Boffy, so softly that nobody heard her. Nobody, that is, except William, Ben and Mary, who were sitting on the carpet close to her feet.

For something quite awful was happening to one of her hands. And Mrs Boffy knew exactly what it was. She was beginning to get pins and needles. And in witches, pins and needles can last for hours. Even days. Not only that . . .

'Oh my dearie me!' whispered Mrs Boffy, as the tingling increased and a shower of tiny shining pins and needles dropped from her finger tips

to stand quivering in Mrs Pitts' blue and orange carpet. 'I wasn't expecting *this*! Raymon Romanski said I'd have trouble with one of my *toes*!'

Very swiftly, before anybody else noticed what was happening, Mrs Boffy said a disappearing spell under her breath. Immediately all the pins and needles vanished. And the new ones that were emerging from her tingling hand, disappeared even before they touched the carpet. It was all very embarrassing. Mrs Boffy hoped that the meeting would soon come to an end.

'We've got to lie down in front of their bulldozers!' cried Miss Peastocking, the school teacher. She had once attended a demonstration where this was done.

'Don't be an idiot, young woman!' cackled Granny Dickens. 'The driver wouldn't even notice you from up there – and *then* where would you be?'

Shuddering, Mary tried not to imagine.

'Well, we've got to do something, isn't it?' cried Mrs Gobowen in desperation.

'Oh dear, can't we just march down Main Street with banners, and post protest leaflets through doors?' asked Reverend Mr Wigglesworth, hopefully. (Needless to say, he had arrived quite properly dressed.)

'No we can NOT!' roared Mrs Pitts. 'People like those at the scrap metal factory take NO NOTICE of leaflets! What we want is ACTION!'

For a minute there was silence. Everybody furiously tried to think. Then Miss Cheeseman said brightly, 'Oh, Mrs Boffy! Can't *you* do something? After all, you are a w–'

'*Cheese*!' exclaimed her mother, just in the nick of time. But it had done the trick. Everybody looked at Mrs Boffy. And tucking her prickling hand behind her back, Mrs Boffy looked at them.

'Well, I'll do my best,' she said mildly. 'But of course, I can't *promise* anything.' (Especially today, she thought.)

Soon after that, the meeting ended. And the three children set off back with Peterkin, Ragtag and Mrs Boffy to Buttercup Cottage.

Chapter Four

THE TROUBLE BEGINS

James was the man from the council. He had been sent to survey the land where they wanted to build the Road. The bit which went right across one of Farmer Dale's fields. To do this, he had a theodolite, which is a kind of telescope balanced upon three long, thin, steel legs. And he was looking through it so intently that he didn't notice when a lady in a floppy tweed hat, three children, a pitch black hat and a greyish-brown donkey hurried past.

But they noticed him.

'Oh my dearie me,' murmured Mrs Boffy. 'I'd better put a stop to this.' And with the little finger and thumb of her right hand she made an extremely magic sign.

But there was something Mrs Boffy didn't know. She didn't know, that far in the distance, another man from the council – a man called Pete – sat in the cabin of his bulldozer, watching and waiting for the signal to begin. The signal from James.

And James bent down to peer through his theodolite. At first, all he could see were trees and fields and an old stone wall. But the next second he went reeling away with a gasp of disbelief. Because all of a sudden, instead of trees and fields and an old stone wall, he saw an eye. An *eye* was looking back at him.

Pulling himself together, James decided to try again. The eye was still there. It was a beautiful eye. Bright blue. Fringed with long, dark, curling lashes. As James stared, transfixed with horror, the eye winked at him. And from somewhere within the theodolite, a voice spoke. A soft, female voice. Which somehow matched the eye. Especially the wink.

'Hallo, gorgeous,' said the velvety voice. 'I've been watching you for simply *ages*. Would you like to dance, darling? I'm afraid I can only do the waltz . . .'

'Aaaaaaaargh!' screamed James. 'Uuuuur, oooooeee!' And waving his arms in the air, he turned and fled.

'Oh, all right then,' said the theodolite sulkily. 'I'll dance by myself.' And it began to waltz stiffly about on its thin tripod legs, humming a little tune.

'Pom pom pom pom POM, pom POM, pom POM!' hummed the theodolite, enjoying itself immensely. But not really looking where it was going. So that suddenly it tripped, and fell into a nearby ditch. And lay still.

Meanwhile, away in the distance, Pete and the bulldozer saw James begin to wave his arms about in a most excited fashion.

'That's it!' exclaimed Pete. 'That's our signal to start the digging! Get to it, me old buddy!'

'Grrrrrrr!' growled the bulldozer as the engine

sprang into life. 'Aaaaaaargh! Rrrrrrrngh! Rrrrrrrnngh! RRRRRRNNNGH!' Which meant, 'OK, Pete, I'm ready for anything!' And swooping down its iron jaws, the bulldozer took an enormous great chunk out of the earth.

'Come along in, my dears,' invited Mrs Boffy, when they arrived back at Buttercup Cottage.

And as they crowded into the neat little parlour, Mary asked, 'Do you think you can do something about the Road?'

'I sincerely hope so,' said Mrs Boffy gravely. 'Because as we were passing the young man with the theodolite, I noticed something I didn't like at all. No, not at all.'

'What was that?' asked William. There was something very interesting coming. He could sense it.

'The bit of land he was surveying,' said Mrs Boffy. 'If they happened to start digging in that *particular* spot . . . well . . . that's why I did a teeny, tiny spell just then. To scare him off. Otherwise, something quite – quite –'

'Quite *what*?' urged Mary and Ben together.

In an absent-minded fashion, Mrs Boffy opened her cupboard and poured out four glasses of pale green mint lemonade. And as she handed them round, the children couldn't help noticing that she kept rubbing her left hand in a rather troubled way.

'Children,' said Mrs Boffy. 'Have you ever stopped to wonder why this village is called Hag's Ditch?'

‘I’ve never actually *wondered*,’ said Mary, cautiously sipping from her glass. ‘But I suppose “hag” is a sort of ancient word, meaning horrible old woman, or wi–’ She stopped suddenly, turning red.

‘That’s right, Mary!’ cried Mrs Boffy, beaming encouragement. ‘“Hag” means witch, and “ditch” means . . . well, exactly what it says!’

‘“Witch’s Ditch”?’ exclaimed Ben, wrinkling his nose as it was attacked by hundreds of mint-flavoured bubbles. ‘You mean, there’s a ditchful of witches somewhere hereabouts?’

‘Exactly!’ said Mrs Boffy. ‘And really wicked pieces of work they are, too! Long, long ago, they plagued the villagers to such an extent that everybody got fed up with them and started to move elsewhere. So in the end, the High Council of Sorcerers decided it was time to act. And the witches were put away.’

'So where are they now?' asked William, although he thought he already knew.

'For a hundred years,' said Mrs Boffy, 'the witches have been imprisoned in a cavern beneath the ground – under a hedge in Farmer Dale's field. And they've been sealed in by the power of a little white flower which grows nowhere else in the whole world. *Meconopsis haegtesse*, or "witch's poppy". While that flower remains, so will the witches. Even if it is picked, more flowers will immediately grow. All the year round. But if the roots are torn out by a bulldozer, nobody knows what might happen.'

Mary clapped a hand over her mouth in horror. 'The witches could get out!'

'They could swarm all over Hag's Ditch again!' breathed Ben, not (it has to be admitted) without a certain amount of excitement.

'This is what I'm afraid of,' frowned Mrs Boffy. 'And although at first they would be rather weak and out of practice, they would gradually gather strength. So that, after a while, say, almost the whole of one day . . . well . . . there could be simply no end to their wickedness!'

Chapter Five

THE CLOUD OF HAGS

While Mrs Boffy was pouring out mint lemonade in Buttercup Cottage, Pete and his bulldozer, Champ, were hard at work. Roaring and graunching, they gobbled their way along the ditch. First of all they demolished a hawthorn hedge where a little brown dunnock had just been planning to build her nest. Then they knocked over part of an ancient wall which, fortunately, a pair of pale and delicate spotted flycatchers, with three spotted babies, had left the previous day.

'Wheeeee!' shouted Pete in delight, as Champ crunched the stones in his great iron teeth. 'Go to it, boy!'

'GggggrrrrrNNNNNGG!' snarled Champ,

breaking the old stile to bits with ease. Suddenly he stopped. Because right in front of him was a great oak. It had been growing in that very spot for five hundred years. It was gigantic! Dozens of different creatures lived within its trunk and among its branches. And around its roots grew a tiny white flower, the like of which grew nowhere else in the world. *Meconopsis haegtesse*. The witch's poppy.

But Pete didn't know that. And if he had known, he wouldn't have cared.

'Come on, Champ! You can do it!' he cried.

'GGRRRRROOOOOW!' roared Champ. And, iron head lowered, he charged.

It took quite a long time to get rid of the oak. But at last, slowly and majestically, it toppled over. The ground shook. And two tawny owls which had been sleeping soundly in a hole in the trunk, flew screeching in alarm to a sweet chestnut on the other side of the field.

'You did it, baby!' shouted Pete. 'Yippee! That was –' He stopped. Because something a bit – sort of – *queer* seemed to be happening just there. Right in the hollow where the oak's great roots had been. A plume of greyish smoke began

rising, spiralling out of the hole. And as it rose into the air, it got denser. And thicker. Forming itself into the shape of a cloud. And as Pete stared in amazement and horror, two great black eyes stared straight at him from inside it!

'H-h-h-help! Ghosties!' yelled Pete. 'Let's get

out of here!' And putting Champ into reverse, he zoomed backwards, all the way across the field. And over the next and the next and even the next, until he reached the busy road, far beyond.

And it was at that particular moment that Peterkin, sitting on the arm of Mrs Boffy's sofa in Buttercup Cottage, did something rather strange. He suddenly drew himself up into a stiff loop, until all his four paws were touching. Then, staring through the window, he hissed sharply. And vanished.

'Look! That's queer!' exclaimed Ben, pointing. Because something was happening in the sky. A great grey cloud was drifting slowly towards them, completely blotting out the sun. And there was something most . . . well, *unusual* about the cloud. It was by no means ordinary. In fact, it seemed to Ben, watching, as if there were things *inside* the cloud. Moving about. And every now and then the edges were broken by what looked very much like a long, thin arm, or a bony leg, or the tip of a pointed hat sticking out. As if some kind of frantic activity were going on inside the cloud. And, just for a moment, Mary was convinced that she glimpsed a face through the greyish mist. A horrid, leering face, with a crooked, warty nose . . .

Peering through the window, they watched the cloud. Slowly it floated over the very middle of Hag's Ditch. And stopped there.

'Whatever is it?' gasped William. They looked at Mrs Boffy. Her expression was very grave.

'It is the Cloud of Hags,' she said solemnly. 'I'm afraid, my dears, that the very worst thing has happened. It is just as I feared. Somehow or other the hags have been released from their ditch. And an infestation of witches is about to begin!'

'Gosh, can you stop them?' asked Ben fearfully. He didn't like the sound of that at all.

'I can try,' said Mrs Boffy bravely. 'But I shall need my wand.'

Mrs Boffy only used her wand upon the very rare occasions when her most powerful magic was needed. And this definitely looked like being one of them. Reaching into the cupboard, she grasped the wand with her left hand.

But as she did so, a sudden, horrid prickling ran right through her fingers. It was so sharp that even the disappearing spell couldn't cope, and a shower of shining pins and needles flew out from under her fingernails.

'Ouch!' exclaimed Mrs Boffy, clenching her hand hard, with the wand in it. CRUNCH!

'Oh!' cried Mrs Boffy in dismay. Slowly she opened her hand, hardly daring to look. But even before she saw it, she knew exactly what had happened to her wand. Raymon Romanski had been right about that!

'It's broken!' cried Mary. And broken it most certainly was. There was a horrid, jagged split right across the middle, and the wand was bent almost in two.

'Botheration and beetles!' groaned Mrs Boffy, staring at the damaged wand.

'What are you going to do now?' asked William anxiously.

'There's only one thing I *can* do,' said Mrs Boffy. 'I shall have to mend it. Wands mend very quickly as a rule, but they need the right conditions. Ben, please go into the kitchen and fetch me a strand of raffia from the onions.'

Ben rushed out of the parlour and came back a few seconds later trailing a long piece of yellow raffia which Mrs Boffy began to wrap tightly

round and round the split in the centre of the wand. Gradually, the wand straightened out.

'It looks much better already!' exclaimed Mary.

'I could do with something to plant it in,' said Mrs Boffy, glancing round. 'William, can you pop just outside and get an empty plant pot?

Mary, I need it half-filled with soil from underneath the apple tree.'

It didn't take long to do.

'And now,' said Mrs Boffy, 'I must have some sand to mix with the soil. And since I haven't got any, I'll just magic a bit on to this piece of newspaper. Please stand clear, children . . .'

It was a good job they did. Almost before Mrs Boffy had finished flicking her fingers – thumpppp! A huge pile of wet and strong-smelling seaweed landed right in the middle, and began dripping salt water all over the carpet. There were even a few surprised fish wriggling about among it.

'My goodness me!' cried Mrs Boffy in horror. '*That's* not right! I'd better try again!'

Another flick of her fingers made the seaweed

disappear. But in its place came something else. Something which most definitely wasn't sand. An enormous blob of what looked like transparent jelly quivered and shook upon the newspaper, and –

'Don't touch it!' shouted Ben, suddenly jumping back. 'It's a tropical jelly-fish! Terribly poisonous!'

'Oh no!' breathed Mrs Boffy. 'It must be these pins and needles! They're making all my magic go wrong. I'm getting everything from the seaside *except* sand! Well, I'll try just once more, but this is the very last time . . .'

'AAAAAAAaaaaaRGH!' The roar came first. It echoed round the parlour, bouncing off the walls and filling the room. Splosh! Slap! Something was trying to materialise on the table.

Something HUGE! Mary screamed, as a pair of great angry red eyes glared down at her from somewhere near the ceiling. Ben gasped in horror as the outline of at least twenty-five humps curled around the walls. And William leapt back as a gaping mouth stretched out towards him.

'Oh, nightjars and natterjacks!' exclaimed Mrs Boffy in exasperation. And before the awful creature had a chance to become anything more substantial than a shadow, she made it disappear again.

'What was it?' shuddered Mary. 'A dragon?'

'No, only a sea-serpent,' said Mrs Boffy. 'There aren't many of them left nowadays. And they're usually quite harmless if left alone.'

'Are you going to try again, Mrs Boffy?' asked Mary, secretly crossing her fingers behind her back for good luck. It worked. Or at least, something did. Because Mrs Boffy was already reaching for her hat.

'Most definitely not, my dear,' she said firmly. 'We will go and ask Grandad Lovell for some. He is a gardener, and gardeners *always* have sand.'

Chapter Six

HAGS ON THE LOOSE

The Cloud of Hags hovered for a while over the middle of Hag's Ditch. Nobody took much notice of it at all. They were used to clouds, anyway. It had been a rotten summer so far that year.

'I do believe it is going to rain again,' said Miss Trickle to Mrs Featherly as they met just outside the supermarket.

'Pour, by the looks of it,' said Mrs Featherly. 'I've never known the clouds to come down *quite* so low before.'

'Perhaps we're in for a storm,' observed Miss Trickle. And nodding pleasantly to each other, they went on their way.

They didn't see the Cloud begin to move. Very quickly, as if a strong wind had suddenly got up and begun to blow it along. It whizzed down Main Street, cutting across the church-yard, and came to rest with a bump in the garden of Number Fourteen Cowslip Lane, which was the house where Granny Dickens lived.

For a few moments the Cloud remained there, swaying slightly. And then, like a flying saucer taking off, it zoomed up into the air . . . leaving somebody behind. A tall, skinny person. A tall, skinny, *grey* person. With grey skimpy hair and grey raggedy clothes and grey wrinkled stock-ings and big grey shoes upon big grey flat feet. Even her face was grey. For a few seconds she stood there. And then she began to walk up the path.

Granny Dickens, in the garden, didn't even notice the Cloud. She was standing upon an upturned bucket with one eye glued to the fence, spying through a knothole on Grandad Lovell next door. She gnashed her teeth in envy as she saw Grandad Lovell stoop down to choose the prize dahlias he was going to put in the Hag's Ditch Flower Show that weekend. They were enormous. They were *beautiful.* The colours were brilliant! They made Granny Dickens dahlias look small, pale and frowsty. He was sure to win!

As Grandad Lovell reached out carefully with his secateurs, Granny Dickens was just wondering what she could do to stop him when she noticed somebody grey walking towards her. She stared in silence as the grey person shambled up to the fence and stood on tiptoe to look over it. Then, pulling a hand out of her pocket, she tossed something across the fence. A kind of fine, grey powder seemed to explode in the air and sprinkle softly down, landing mostly on Grandad Lovell.

He straightened up as, all of a sudden, he was covered from head to foot in grey dust. And he looked very, very cross. He whirled round and round on the spot. He shook his fists in the air.

He snapped his secateurs. And he positively sizzled with rage! Glaring down at his prize dahlias he shouted, 'Too much pollen! You stupid flowers! I've looked after you for weeks and weeks, and you've made too much pollen! You'll never win that prize now!'

And bending down he began snipping furiously to right and left. Chopping off the heads of his beautiful dahlias until every one of them lay on the ground. Useless. Leaves and petals strewn everywhere.

Granny Dickens' mouth dropped open as she watched. She turned to the grey person in surprise and delight.

'How did you do that?' she asked.

'Easy-peasy!' chuckled the hag.

Granny Dickens took one last satisfied look through her knothole. Then she stepped down from the bucket.

'Come along in, my dear,' she said sweetly to the hag. 'I'm *sure* you would like a nice cup of tea!'

'Crumbs, did you see that?' whispered Ben. They had arrived just in time to work out what was happening. Mrs Boffy nodded grimly.

'He's totally bewitched,' she said, as Grandad Lovell began tearing up the headless green stalks of his dahlias by the roots and throwing them up in the air. 'We'll never get any sand from him now.'

'What about the supermarket? We could try there,' suggested William. 'They've got a gardening section, and they might have a little bag of sand.'

'That's a good idea, William,' said Mrs Boffy. 'But we must hurry!'

At about the very same time Mrs Pitts was standing in front of the mirror in her hall, putting on her most intimidating hat. She was on her way out to visit the managing director of the scrap metal factory to give him a piece of her mind. She would tell him *exactly* what she thought of his idea to put a Road right through the middle of Hag's Ditch. And while she was about it, she would also tell him what she thought of his factory, the people who worked there, the members of the council, and *especially* the managing director himself. And she would enjoy every minute of it.

Which was why Mrs Pitts was especially annoyed when there was a knock on her front door. Irritably she opened it, to see a grey person standing there. A dusty, raggedy, grey person, with a long hooked nose and a pointed chin.

'Oh!' said Mrs Pitts, stepping slightly back. 'No tramps, thank you! No gipsies, no collectors, no cat food questionnaires, and definitely *no* double glazing!'

'And *that* to you,' said the hag rudely, whipping one hand from behind her back and squirting something from a grey bag right into Mrs Pitts' face.

Mrs Pitts gasped. She coughed and spluttered. She choked and wheezed.

'How *dare* you?' screamed Mrs Pitts at last, fumbling for a hanky to wipe the grey powder from her eyes. 'Get out of my house, you frightful, nasty old –' And Mrs Pitts waved her arms to shoo the hag away.

She slammed the front door, and she was just turning to the mirror to adjust her hat, when something rather annoying began to happen. As she reached up, both of her arms suddenly went stiff. Stiff as pokers.

'That wretched rheumatism again!' snapped Mrs Pitts. She struggled to put her arms down again, but found to her annoyance that they wouldn't move. And to make matters worse, both her legs had seized up as well.

'Oh my goodness!' croaked Mrs Pitts in alarm. 'Whatever is happening to m-m-m-mmm . . .' She stopped. Because at that very moment her tongue wouldn't work any more. Neither would her fingers, or her toes, or even her eyelashes. She couldn't move her head either, no matter how hard she tried. And Mrs Pitts *did* try. Because she was still looking into the mirror, and there she saw a perfectly horrid sight.

Very gradually, every bit of her seemed to be

turning to stone. Pale grey stone. Even the large yellow velvet flowers on her hat. And as Mrs Pitts stared in horror at her grey, stony reflection, she saw something which filled her with even greater dread.

Little splits had begun to appear in her cheeks, and were spreading upwards to her forehead and down into her neck. And suddenly, as she watched, there was a sharp crack as the tip of her nose broke off and dropped to the floor.

Mrs Pitts couldn't do anything. She couldn't run, or bend, or blink, or scream, or even cry. And as she stood like a statue, the front door swung open and a great grey Cloud drifted in.

Chapter Seven

STRANGE SWEETS AND CURIOUS CAKES

Mrs Drewitt was in the kitchen of her little shop, concocting a delicious new sweet.

'Now, let's see,' she mused, examining her tray of ingredients. 'A little sprinkle of coconut, I think. And some pink icing sugar. And perhaps a dash of –'

Just then, the shop bell tinkled and Miss Drewitt hurried out to serve the customer.

'Oh!' said Miss Drewitt in astonishment, because she really had expected to see somebody she knew. Somebody from the village. Like Mrs Gobowen, or Miss Cheeseman, or Mr Howell the churchwarden. What she did *not* expect to see was a tall, grey lady. Looking a bit dusty. In fact, very dusty. As if a film of cobwebs were covering her from head to foot.

'Oh,' said Miss Drewitt again. Then, not wanting to appear rude, she smiled and said politely, 'Can I help you?'

'Not nearly as much as I can help you, dearie,' said the grey hag, giving a wide, jagged leer. Even her teeth were grey.

'H – how do you mean?' asked Miss Drewitt nervously.

'I've come to try and interest you in a delicious new sweet,' said the hag in her most persuasive tone. 'Created in my own home. The likes of these you've never tasted before. Here. Try one.'

Opening her hand, the hag showed Miss Drewitt something which looked like a grey pebble. Miss Drewitt stared. And gulped. Then she said doubtfully, 'Well, I'm really not sure . . . it's rather an unusual colour . . .'

'Colour's got nothing to do with it!' snapped the hag. 'As you very well know! It's what's *inside* that counts.'

Miss Drewitt didn't know what to do. To tell the truth, she was becoming more anxious by the minute. She wished hard that somebody would walk into the shop, preferably PC Starling. He would soon send this horrid old woman packing, with her ghastly sweet.

But he didn't come. Neither did anyone else.

'Go on, what are you waiting for?' urged the hag. So poor Miss Drewitt reached out and took the sweet. First she sniffed it. Really, it didn't smell half as bad as it looked. Cautiously she nibbled at one corner. Oh! How scrumptious! How *gorgeous*!

In a trice, Miss Drewitt had popped the whole sweet in her mouth and started to chew. As the delicious taste flooded over her tongue, she began to wonder briefly what the ingredients could be. Just for a second or two, she wondered. And then, quite suddenly, Miss Drewitt didn't wonder any more. Because she had other things on her mind.

All of a sudden, something very peculiar had begun to happen. It was the sweet in her mouth that was the cause of the trouble. At first it was quite lovely, and Miss Drewitt chewed it very slowly, because she wanted to make it last. But far from dwindling in size, the more she chewed the sweet, the bigger it seemed to get. And the

bigger it got, the more gooey it became. So that soon Miss Drewitt was having to work like mad to keep her teeth from being totally stuck together. Watching her, the hag cackled with evil glee.

'Oooogle booogle glub!' mumbled Miss Drewitt as the sweet covered her entire tongue and pressed against the roof of her mouth.

'Aaaah, aaaaagh uggle GOO!' gasped Miss Drewitt in desperation, as the swelling sweet forced her mouth open wide. Digging her finger into the middle of the awful mess she pulled some of it out and tried to throw it away. But the sweet clung to her hands and glued her fingers together.

As she was fighting to get them free, the telephone rang suddenly. Miss Drewitt lurched towards it and dragged the receiver off the hook. Oh, thank goodness! If only she could tell somebody what was happening! They would surely get Dr Pigeon straight away. Or PC Starling, or the Fire Brigade, or . . . *anybody* . . .

'Ugg guggle GLUGG!' screamed Miss Drewitt into the phone.

'Oh, I'm dreadfully sorry,' said the phone in a surprised voice. 'I wanted to speak to Miss Drewitt, but I must have the wrong number.' And it rang off.

Gasping in despair, Miss Drewitt staggered to the door and somehow dragged it open. Then she stumbled down the steps and sank down on to the pavement as strands of sweet curled themselves around her wrists and reached down towards her ankles.

And she was struggling so desperately to escape that she didn't even see the huge grey Cloud rolling purposefully towards her, along the street.

The children at the village school were not due to

start their holiday for another three days. And Miss Peastocking was just beginning a nature study lesson when the door opened and an old, grey lady walked in.

Miss Peastocking looked up in surprise for a moment. Then she smiled.

'Oh, good morning! You must be John Birtwistle's nanny, come to help us with the baking! And how is poor John? I do hope his measles are almost better!'

'Haaaaaahmmmm,' grunted the old lady, which as a reply, was neither here nor there, really. But Miss Peastocking didn't notice. She was already checking the register to see whose turn it was.

'Now here we are, the next people to do baking are Jane Harrison, Paul Pincher, and Delia Anstruther. Off you go, and show John's nanny where all the equipment is kept – and mind you make something really exciting, now!'

'Hhhhmmmmheerrummm,' agreed the hag, following the children from the room. Miss Peastocking watched them go. And noticing the hag's raggedy old skirt and a great hole in her stocking, she couldn't help thinking that John

Birtwistle's nanny was rather *weird*.

It wasn't five minutes before they were back. 'Well, my word, you were quick!' exclaimed Miss Peastocking. To tell the truth, she was a little bit miffed. She hadn't even finished the nature lesson yet.

Delia Anstruther carefully carried a wire tray upon which thirty-five tiny cakes were steaming. Miss Peastocking gazed at them doubtfully. They certainly didn't *look* very appetising. They were quite a peculiar colour, too. She had certainly never seen *grey* cakes before. She took the tray from Delia, and sniffed. And immediately her expression changed to one of amazement and delight.

'Oh! What a perfectly delicious smell!' she exclaimed. 'Children, I'm sure we're going to *love* these! I know, let's eat them straight away while they're still warm! Delia, you hold the tray while Paul gives them out. No, Daniel, don't even *touch* yours yet! We'll wait until *everybody* has been served.'

At last, everybody had one of the little grey cakes. Including Miss Peastocking. Everybody, that is, except the hag. She hadn't made one for herself.

'Right!' sang out Miss Peastocking at last. 'Now we can have our treat!'

It was lovely and quiet in the classroom. Contentedly, the children and Miss Peastocking bit into their cakes, which were so mouth-watering that they were soon finished down to the very last crumb.

'That was really quite de . . .' began Miss Peastocking, turning to the hag. But, before she could finish the sentence, her eyes closed and she slumped down in her chair. Fast asleep. Snoring gently. And the children didn't even laugh, or look surprised, or anything. Because they were asleep already.

Chapter Eight

THE TERRIBLE SWARM

One or two people couldn't help staring at the tall, thin, grey lady who shuffled round the supermarket. She was very peculiar. Because instead of taking things *off* the shelves to put into her wire basket, she seemed to be doing it the other way round. She was putting things back. But on all the wrong shelves.

Her basket was full of long, shiny, silver-grey tins covered with large white letters which said ZAPP THAT FLY! And underneath was a picture of a fly lying on its back with its legs in the air. But tins of fly spray don't belong clanking among the cat food. Or bashing against the biscuits. Or squashing the sausages. Or rolling over the rhubarb. But that is where they were.

'How very strange, my dear!' whispered Miss Trickle to Mrs Gobowen as they stood and watched. Trying hard not to *stare*, of course, because that would have been rather rude.

'I wonder what on earth she's doing it for, look you?' murmured Mrs Gobowen. 'Surely, and indeed to goodness, she can't be a new kind of saleslady?'

'You never know,' muttered Miss Trickle. 'Perhaps it's just a new gimmick invented by the makers of ZAPP.'

Indeed, by now, everybody in the supermarket was either whispering about the hag, or else picking up the tins of ZAPP to examine them closely. Which meant that nobody was actually *buying* anything. So it wasn't long before the manager arrived.

'Will you please explain what you are doing, madam?' he asked in a very huffy voice.

'Just looking,' answered the hag vaguely, grinning an evil grey grin.

'I see,' said the manager. 'Well, I should be glad if you would please leave. NOW! And give me that basket!'

He snatched the basket from the hag. By now it was empty. Without a word the hag ambled away, through the electronic doors and out of sight. But she didn't go far. Just around the corner, she stopped. And waited. And no sooner had she gone than the supermarket seemed to be filled with a strange buzzing sound.

'Good gracious!' exclaimed Miss Trickle. 'Is that a fly I can hear, Mrs Gobowen?'

'If there's only one, it's very large indeed, look you!' cried Mrs Gobowen, staring round in alarm. 'Oh, oh! Ohhhhhh!'

Screaming shrilly, Miss Trickle and Mrs Gobowen ducked down in horror as they were suddenly dive-bombed by about two and a half million flies. Flies of all descriptions. Blowflies and gadflies, botflies and harvest-flies, horse-flies and window-flies, house-flies, hover-flies, soldier-flies and robber-flies – in fact, every kind of fly which has ever been heard of and even one or two which have not. Ugh! They were horrible! They turned the air black! The noise was INCREDIBLE.

They flew into people's faces and clung to their clothes. They tickled their ears and walked around in their hair. Mingled with the awful buzzing were the shrieks and screams of the customers and staff. Some people immediately headed for the doorway. But they found to their horror that, somehow or other, the doors had become jammed and wouldn't open. So they had to run back again.

And then they suddenly remembered the tins of ZAPP. Pouncing and pushing, they snatched the tins and began to spray. In a trice, the supermarket was filled with the sound of hissing aerosols. The lady at the cash till was so nervous that she turned hers the wrong way round and sprayed herself by mistake.

'Go away! Take that – AND THAT!' shrieked Miss Trickle, squeezing the trigger and aiming into the swarm.

'Oh, what a lovely smell, dear,' said Mrs Gobowen suddenly, as the spray drifted gently down around them. 'Violets, surely!'

'No, freesias,' said Miss Trickle, lowering the tin. 'Yes, definitely freesias.'

And then, all at once, Miss Trickle's expression changed to one of alarm. She put out a hand, as if to steady herself.

'Oh my goodness me!' she exclaimed. 'I don't know whether it is my allergy to dogs, or whether I'm sickening for something, but all of a sudden I feel very *dizzy*! Can you see a dog about anywhere?'

Miss Trickle sounded so distressed that Mrs Gobowen looked around quickly, ready to shoo away any dog which might have wandered into the supermarket. But there wasn't one to be seen.

'Oh, oh!' wailed Miss Trickle, beginning to sway dangerously from side to side. 'Please may I hold on to you, Mrs Gobowen?'

'Of course, look you . . .' began Mrs Gobowen, as Miss Trickle clutched at her arm. Then she stopped. Because something very peculiar seemed to be happening to the supermarket floor. It seemed to be moving. So did the shelves and the windows and the customers, not to mention Mrs Gobowen herself. Everything and everybody was swaying and spinning, round and round. It was most worrying.

'I'm afraid I'm beginning to feel quite . . .' murmured Mrs Gobowen, putting one hand to her head and reaching the other towards a shelf which refused to keep still. 'Oh! Oh . . . HELP!'

And before she could do anything to save herself, Mrs Gobowen tripped backwards into the big vegetable rack, landing right in the middle of the salads. The more she struggled to get up, the deeper she sank down among the lettuces, celery, boiled beetroot, spring onions and tomatoes. Until at last, weak and panting from the awful effort, she stopped struggling and lay still.

Miss Trickle didn't even notice what was happening to Mrs Gobowen. She was too busy. Because at the very moment when Mrs Gobowen had fallen into the salad, Miss Trickle had reeled across towards the herbs and spices. THUMP! Head spinning, she cannoned heavily against the stand and hurtled to the ground. Clunk, CRACK! As the stand toppled over beside her, there came the sound of splintering jars and crushed lids. And the cloves clattered and peppercorns popped like mad as Miss Trickle scrabbled around in a desperate attempt to get to her feet.

But by now the floor was so slippery with little round things rolling about that the moment Miss Trickle tried to stand up, her feet shot from under her and she fell straight down again. Not only that, but most of the jars had lost their lids, and clouds of strong-smelling powder were puffing into the air.

'Oh!' gasped Miss Trickle, as a stream of turmeric shot across under her nose, making her

head spin even more. 'Oh! Ah, oo, get away!' Eyes watering horribly, she waved her hands about and tried to clear the air. But the turmeric was followed immediately by apple-pie spice, mixed with orange paprika and black pepper. So that Miss Trickle's eyes started watering all over again. Even worse.

'Boo-hooo! Waaaaah!' sobbed Miss Trickle, sitting down hard upon the floor. And this time she was so exhausted, that she didn't even bother trying to get up. And neither she nor Mrs Gobowen knew, nor cared a single jot, that everywhere else in the supermarket all the customers were spinning dizzily around. Until, with faint cries of dismay, they toppled one by one into the display shelves, then collapsed helplessly upon the ground as the tins and jars and boxes clattered down about them.

It was at that precise moment that Mrs Boffy, Ben, William and Mary, with Ragtag and Peterkin trotting behind them, turned into Main Street. And hardly had they taken half a dozen steps towards the supermarket, than a most extraordinary thing happened.

A great, grey Cloud swooped suddenly down from the sky, landing right outside the electronic doors. The doors swished open and the Cloud rolled swiftly through. Mrs Boffy, the three children, Ragtag and Peterkin stopped in their tracks.

'I don't like the look of *that*,' said Mrs Boffy, shaking her head. 'Not at all. Not one little bit, my dears.' And she had scarcely finished speaking when the doors sprang open once more, and the Cloud meandered out into Main Street.

'Hurry!' whispered Mrs Boffy urgently. 'Up Sparrow Hill, before it spots *us*!' And dodging across the street they ran thankfully into the safety of the narrow lane.

Chapter Nine

WHERE HAVE ALL THE CHILDREN GONE?

'It's no good expecting to get sand from the supermarket now,' exclaimed Mrs Boffy in exasperation as they slowed down to a walk. 'Let's stop and think for a minute, children.'

Everybody thought hard. Then Mary suddenly cried, 'I know! What about the school? In ours they have a sand-tray in every one of the infants' classrooms!'

'How clever of you!' beamed Mrs Boffy. 'I certainly would never have remembered that, my dear!'

'EeeeeHAAAW!' agreed Ragtag.

Keeping a sharp look out for any of the supermarket crowd, they hurried back into Main Street. And, as they rounded the corner, a perfectly horrid sight met their eyes. Because, at the other end of the street, resting on the ground right outside the school, was the Cloud of Hags.

'Oh no!' breathed Mrs Boffy in dread. 'I don't like the look of that! Those hags are up to no good again! And the children are still there! They haven't broken up for the holidays yet!'

'Perhaps the hags don't know –' began Ben hopefully, when suddenly, something began to happen to the Cloud. It started to quiver and shake all over. Like a great grey dollop of mousse gone wrong. And then, very very slowly indeed, as if there were an enormous weight inside it, the Cloud lifted off and started to float away.

It was so heavy that it scarcely cleared the rooftops. And bits of it were left behind, clinging mistily to Miss Drewitt's chimney-pot.

'Quick!' cried Miss Boffy. 'We've got to warn everybody in the school before the Cloud comes back!'

So with Ragtag clattering behind on his tiny hooves and Peterkin bounding in front, they dashed up Main Street and soon arrived, furiously panting, at the gates of the school.

'Who shall we tell first?' asked Ben. He wasn't really sure that he liked the idea, after all. Schools were funny places, sometimes. You might get told off, in fact, by the very people you were trying to help.

'It doesn't matter!' exclaimed Mary. 'Just grab anybody who'll listen to you!'

Which was easier said than done. Because at first glance, it seemed as if nobody was there. Nobody that is, who *should* have been. But plenty who shouldn't. *Hags*.

There were six in Miss Peastocking's classroom. One of them was the hag she had mistaken for John Birtwistle's nanny. And *she* was behaving in a most disgraceful way. One by one she was going through all the drawers in the children's lockers, and tossing the contents around the room. Papers and books and crayons and pencils and rubbers and rulers and badges and pictures and little cards and birthday invitations and *everything* went flying up into the air, to land on the ground in a dreadful muddle. And all the time she was doing it, the hag screamed with laughter!

'Oh!' gasped Mary, clasping a hand over her mouth. 'Oh, how awful!'

Another hag was scribbling over the blackboard in coloured chalks. Quite covering Miss Peastocking's beautifully set out sums. Another was tearing down the paintings and throwing

them into a wastepaper basket, where she stamped on them gleefully with enormous flat feet. Another was writing on the clean yellow walls with Miss Peastocking's purple felt-tip pen. Rude things, like, 'Teachers are all wallies' and 'Children should be neither seen nor heard'.

'They're nuts!' whispered William, turning quite pale. 'Come on, let's get out of here!'

They crept past the other classrooms where the same kind of mayhem was taking place. And past the headmaster's study, where a hag sat with her feet up on his table, smoking his favourite pipe. Another was in the staff room playing with the secretary's typewriter, bashing the keys so hard that the letters flew off the ends.

'Oh my stars and goodness!' whispered Mrs Boffy. 'This is far worse than anything I could have imagined!'

'And where have all the children gone?' wailed Mary.

'Something has happened to them,' said Ben in a low voice.

William nodded. 'Something very bad,' he said gravely. 'Connected with that bloomin' Cloud, I reckon.'

'Yes,' agreed Mrs Boffy. 'Did you notice what a job it had to lift off the ground?'

'As if it were full up with . . . well . . . full up with . . .' said Ben slowly. He couldn't finish the sentence. He was beginning to feel very creepy. As if, for instance, about sixteen spiders were crawling up his neck, into his hair.

'Something . . . or *somebody*,' shuddered William.

'You mean . . . *people*?' breathed Mary. For a moment they stared at one another in horror.

'Come on!' cried Mrs Boffy. 'Let's find out who else they've kidnapped in that Cloud!'

They were in such a rush to get out of the school that they almost forgot the sand. But just at the last moment, as they were passing the nursery, Ben noticed some in a big tray standing near the door. There were three witches having goes on the slide, but they were so busy screaming and shrieking and pushing and quarrelling that they didn't see Ben reach inside to grab a big handful. He stuffed it into his trouser pocket and fled.

With Ragtag and Peterkin hard behind them, they rushed down Main Street. Everywhere they looked, there were hags. Making mischief. Two of them were in the sweet shop tasting Miss Drewitt's sweets, eating everything they liked and throwing the rest on the floor. And in Dr Pigeon's surgery, the outline of a tall, pointed hat could be seen through frosted glass.

Hurrying past, they went towards the supermarket. Before they had even got anywhere near it, they could hear the hags inside. Shrieks and yells and bursts of shrill laughter mingled with the smash and crash of falling glass, the crunch of breaking biscuits, the squelch of squashing fruit and the thuds and thumps of various sized tins, as hags hurled things down the aisles.

'They'll destroy the whole village at this rate!' cried Mary. 'What on earth can we do?'

'We've got to get Mrs Boffy's wand repaired!' exclaimed Ben. 'Look, here's some sand! I hope it's enough!'

'Ben, you are an absolute marvel!' praised Mrs Boffy in delight. 'That will be plenty! Come on, back to Buttercup Cottage – there's no time to be lost!'

Chapter Ten

FOLLOW THAT CLOUD!

Hoping they wouldn't meet any more hags on the way, Mrs Boffy, the three children, Ragtag and Peterkin rushed back to the cottage. And the moment the door was safely shut behind them, Mrs Boffy set to work mixing Ben's sand with the soil in the flowerpot. And as she worked, she whispered a little spell, very softly, under her breath, so that nobody but Peterkin could hear the words.

It wasn't long before she had finished. And she was just about to plant the wand, when Mary gave a sudden squeal. Everybody stared as she pointed to the window. And froze in horror. Ben and William leapt across to look.

Because coming up the garden path was a tall, skinny grey person. On her grey, skimpy hair she wore a tall grey hat with a crooked point. And a big grey wart grew upon the side of her sharp, grey nose.

'Quick!' exclaimed Mrs Boffy grimly. 'Out of the back door, everybody. Ragtag, you as well. Peterkin, stay with me. *We'll* deal with this!'

'Weeeeeiaooow!' agreed Peterkin eagerly, green eyes agleam.

'And keep an eye on that Cloud for me, children!' called Mrs Boffy as she bundled them out into the back garden and shut the door.

Well, Ben didn't want to. But squaring his shoulders and lifting his chin he said bravely, 'Come on. Let's go and find that rotten old Cloud.'

'Eeeeee-ahuuuuuh!' snorted Ragtag, pawing the ground.

So, with the little donkey skittering behind, William, Ben and Mary raced back along Main Street to where they had last seen the Cloud of Hags.

'It looked so *heavy*!' panted Mary. 'I'm sure it can't move very fast now!'

'You're right,' puffed William. 'We must be able to catch up with it soon!'

'Come on, this way!' cried William, pointing beyond the school. 'Straight through the playground and over the hedge into Farmer Dale's fields. There's nothing to stop us now!'

It was true. On the way they passed PC Starling's bicycle lying in the gutter, wheels spinning slowly. And they passed the Cheesemans' ponies tethered to a lamp-post, their saddles quite empty.

And, although they didn't know it, not very far away in the farmhouse kitchen Mrs Dale was busy making a cake. But with most *unusual* results. It had all started when she opened a brand new bag of flour. Flour delivered by a rather strange-looking driver. Flour of a most peculiar colour. Grey.

'Well,' said Mrs Dale, eyeing the flour doubtfully. 'I suppose it must be a different make, that's all. Something to do with leaving in the good stuff and leaving out all the nasty chemicals.'

So, having convinced herself that it was all right, she seized the bag, ready to begin. But hardly had Mrs Dale started to measure the flour into her scales than something weird happened. Before she could turn away, or rush to get a hanky, Mrs Dale gave a most enormous SNEEZE. Right *into* the flour. It went *everywhere*. Practically the whole lot left the scales and shot up into the air. Then it came down again. And most of it landed on Mrs Dale – her face, her hair, and worst of all, it tickled her nose unbearably, so that she sneezed once more.

'Oh!' cried Mrs Dale. 'Oh my dearie me! Sneezing? But I haven't got a –' She flapped her hands in distress, hardly noticing that, as she did so, one of her hands caught the flour bag and swept it to the floor with a whump!

And then, Mrs Dale stopped. She stared round nervously. Because all of a sudden, in the quiet kitchen, she heard a very strange noise. Mrs Dale listened hard. It had only just started, of that she was sure. It hadn't been there a moment ago. And it was very, very creepy. As if somebody were . . . well . . . *breathing*. Somebody else, that is, besides herself.

Feeling more than a bit scared, Mrs Dale looked wildly about. It wasn't the cat. He was in the barn searching for mice. Or sleeping, more likely. And it wasn't her. *She* didn't make that wheezy, dusty, *floury* kind of sound when she . . .

Mrs Dale gazed down. Her eyes popped. Her mouth dropped open in a terrified squeak. And she jumped backwards, staring in horror. Because something was happening to the bag of flour. It wasn't just lying there any more, as an ordinary bag of flour will do when it's just been knocked to the floor. It was *moving*. To be exact, it was *breathing*. Panting. Its paper sides were huffing in and out, and little puffs of grey flour were coming from its open mouth.

'Uhuh, uhuh, uhuh,' whispered the flour bag. And as Mrs Dale watched in terror, the bag began to shuffle around on its middle until its horrid, panting mouth was completely turned towards Mrs Dale.

And then the bag began to edge towards her. Wriggling along like a great, grey, paper slug, leaving little patches of flour on the red quarry tiles. Mrs Dale froze to the spot, while the grey flour slug got nearer and nearer, its mouth stretching open like a snake about to swallow an egg.

And of course, Mrs Dale didn't even think to

glance at the open window. So she never even saw the huge, dense Cloud that was squeezing through it into the kitchen, to rise up behind her.

There was a gap in the hedge. And no sooner had Mary squeezed through it than she dodged back again. She crouched down, waving to the others to do the same.

'Look!' she hissed, because there was the Cloud. In front of them, but some little distance away. It was moving very sluggishly now. Every now and again it would bump on the ground before floating a few more metres.

'Oh gosh!' gasped Ben in sudden horror. 'I'm sure I saw Mrs Pitts' hat just then, sticking out of the Cloud!'

'Right, let's go!' exclaimed William. 'Everybody, keep down low, and don't let them see you!'

Almost on hands and knees among the buttercups, the three children crept along. Peterkin plodded behind them, stopping every now and again with his head lowered, pretending to be a rock, or a large bush.

'It's gone into the next field,' whispered Ben,

craning his neck above the long grass to see. 'The one where they're planning to build the Road!'

'And where the Ditch lies buried – or did!' gasped Mary.

'Quick, we've got to get there before – before –' William didn't quite know what. But he had the strongest feeling that something quite awful was about to happen if they – or *somebody* – didn't stop it.

Standing up, running hard, the children headed for the next field. Pushing through a weak spot in the hedge, they emerged on the other side. A scene of terrible ruin met their eyes. There was the great and ancient oak, lying on its side. The stone wall had been crunched into tiny fragments. The stile was a pile of splinters. And underneath, where the roots of the oak had been . . .

Crouched under the hedge, the children peered round. There was no sign of the Cloud. It was safe to go nearer. Telling Ragtag to stay out of sight among the long grass, the three children crept towards the Ditch. And at last they reached the edge. Staring down, they shuddered at what they saw.

Far below them was the mouth of a great, dark cavern. And just in front of the cavern was a huge boulder which had been rolled away. The cavern was empty.

'Whew!' whistled William. 'So that's where they came from!'

'And that's where they're probably planning to dump everybody else when they take over Hag's Ditch!' breathed Mary.

Suddenly, and he didn't yet know why, the hairs on the back of Ben's neck began to tingle. And a funny feeling crept right over the top of his head. Which, as everybody knows, is a warning that something rather nasty might be about to happen. It is a warning of danger. Danger close by . . .

Ben whirled round. There was the Cloud. Right behind him. So close that he could have reached out and pushed his fingers into it. So close that he could actually see the faint outline of Farmer Dale's boots near the edge, and a pointed, wrinkled face peering through the mist. Leering at him with a triumphant kind of grin. Because the Cloud was edging closer. Another few seconds and he, William and Mary would be right inside!

Chapter Eleven

MRS BOFFY'S JUST IN TIME!

'Quick, RUN!' yelled Ben at the top of his voice, dodging sideways just in time. With gasps of horror the children began to run back across the field towards the hedge. And glancing fearfully over their shoulders, they could see the Cloud following them. Scudding along the ground as if blown by a gusty wind.

'Keep going!' panted Mary as they neared the gap in the hedge. Ben didn't know if he could. He was beginning to get the stitch, and might have to stop in a minute to touch his toes . . .

'Come ON!' shouted William. Together they hurled themselves through the gap. Surely now they were safe? They turned to look. And, to their horror, they saw the Cloud rise in the air and float over the hedge towards them!

'Keep running!' cried William.

'Oh crumbs!' gasped Ben, gripping his side. The stitch was getting worse. Threatening to slow him down. And all the while the Cloud was getting closer . . . closer . . .

'Ben, hurry UP!' shrieked Mary. She ran back to catch his hand.

'Stitch!' groaned Ben, almost doubled in two.

It was no good. He would simply have to stop. But the others needn't get caught because of him.

'You go on,' he whispered hoarsely, prepared to sink to the ground and let the Cloud swallow him up.

‘Don’t be stupid!’ screamed Mary. ‘William, quick! We’ve got to get him on to Ragtag’s back!’

It was a marvellous idea. And it worked. With Ben on his back, clinging to his bristly mane, Ragtag fairly scampered through the long grass. He soon drew away from the others, far out of reach of the menacing Cloud.

Leaving the field and the Cloud and Mary and William far behind them, Ben and Ragtag galloped down Main Street past the school. Soon

they turned sharply into Buttercup Lane and hurtled through Mrs Boffy's front gate. Sliding swiftly off Ragtag's back, Ben hammered the door like mad. In a trice it was opened and Mrs Boffy stood there, beaming.

'Ben!' she cried. 'Come and have a look at my wand! It's almost –' She broke off, a puzzled frown spreading across her face. 'But why are you on your own? Where are the others?'

As Ben hurried into Mrs Boffy's parlour, he told her the dreadful news about the Cloud.

'Then there's absolutely no time to be lost,' declared Mrs Boffy. 'We must get to work right away!'

'But what about your wand?' asked Ben anxiously. 'Is it ready to use?'

'We shall soon find out,' said Mrs Boffy. 'Everybody in the Cloud is in great danger, Ben. The hags are becoming more powerful by the minute. We mustn't let them get that Cloud back into the Ditch!'

As she spoke, Mrs Boffy snapped her fingers. And with a rustle of twigs, her broomstick rose from its place in the hearth and swished through the air to stand, hovering, in front of them.

'Quick, get on!' urged Mrs Boffy.

What, me? thought Ben. But he didn't say it. Because quick as a flash, Peterkin leapt up to sit amongst the twigs, disappearing as he went. Gathering up her skirts, Mrs Boffy perched behind him on the handle. And, fearful of being left behind, Ben jumped astride the broomstick, hanging for dear life to Mrs Boffy's apron-strings.

'Go, broomstick, FLY!' shouted Mrs Boffy.

'Prrrrrrriaooow!' echoed Peterkin, from somewhere near the front.

'Wo-ow-ooow!' yelled Ben, as they turned towards the chimney and dived inside.

They were making for Buttercup Cottage. Mary and William panted and gasped as they ran, ran, ran, ran. Their legs were aching and they were short of breath. Both of them could actually feel the cold, damp tendrils of cloud touching their necks. They could see soft little grey swirls in front of their eyes. They could *feel* the weight of the Cloud above them, ready to –

And then, quite suddenly, it happened. The Cloud wasn't there any more. It simply *wasn't*

there. One moment it was all around them, like fog. And the next moment – gone. The children stopped running. As they stared round, the sun came out. And there, in front of them, just stepping down from her broomstick, was Mrs Boffy. Wand in hand. And hopping off behind her was . . . Ben!

'Ben!' squealed Mary. 'Did you *really* ride on Mrs Boffy's broomstick?'

'Wow! What was it like?' breathed William.

'I'll tell you later, when I get my breath back,' puffed Ben. But there was a great big grin on his face, all the same.

'My word, it looks as if we were just in time,' smiled Mrs Boffy.

'Meeeeeeiaow!' agreed Peterkin, materialising bit by bit on the grass beside her. He'd decided to take no chances until the Cloud of Hags had vanished completely.

'Oh, you were!' cried William. 'We're really glad to see you, Mrs Boffy!'

'And thank you for keeping an eye on things,' said Mrs Boffy with a twinkle.

'And the hags?' Even as he asked the question, William felt he knew the answer already.

'In the Ditch where they belong,' said Mrs Boffy with satisfaction. 'And all the villagers are where *they* should be, too. Not remembering anything.' She hesitated. 'That is, all except the scrap metal factory owner and his wife. They were both captured by the Cloud, and didn't like it one little bit. So I've left them just enough memory to be sure that the Road won't go through Hag's Ditch. If they ever build one at all, after this.'

Taking one last look behind them, the children could see the great oak standing in its proper place as if nothing had ever happened. So were the stile and the hedgerow and the old stone wall. Later that evening, the tawny owls would be able to return. And underneath the oak tree bloomed the tiny *Meconopsis haegtesse*, witch's poppy, sealing in the hags for ever. Unless, of course, the unexpected happened. As it is ever likely to do. Especially in Hag's Ditch.

At Number Fourteen Cowslip Lane, Granny Dickens returned from the kitchen carrying two cups of tea, to find that her new friend wasn't there any more. The chair in which the grey person had been sitting was empty. And there was nobody else in the room.

'What a pity,' said Granny Dickens to herself. 'Just when we were getting along so well.'

Suddenly she caught sight of something on the carpet. It was a little pile of grey dust. Quickly, Granny Dickens swept it into a bag.

'Hmmm,' she grinned, as she put the bag of dust carefully away in a drawer. 'Very useful stuff, that. Never know when it might come in handy again!'

Also by Jo Furminger

A SPELL FOR MISS GRIMSCUTTLE
MRS BOFFY'S BIRTHDAY
OH NO, AUNT BELLADONNA!
A GHOST FOR MISS GRIMSCUTTLE
HURRY HOME, MRS BOFFY!